A Gift
from

FRIENDS
OF THE
PALO ALTO
LIBRARY

CONTENTS

VOL. 18
Action Edition

Story and Art by
RUMIKO TAKAHASHI

English Adaptation by Gerard Jones

Translation/Mari Morimoto
Touch-Up Art & Lettering/Bill Schuch
Cover and Interior Graphics & Design/Yuki Ameda
Editor/Avery Gotoh
Supervising Editor/Michelle Pangilinan

Managing Editor/Annette Roman
Editor in Chief/Alvin Lu
Production Manager/Noboru Watanabe
Sr. Dir. of Licensing and Acquisitions/Rika Inouye
VP of Sales/Joe Morici
VP of Marketing/Liza Coppola
Executive VP/Hyoe Narita
Publisher/Seiji Horibuchi

Printed in Canada.

Published by VIZ, LLC
P.O. Box 77010
San Francisco, CA 94107

Action Edition
10 9 8 7 6 5 4 3 2
First printing, June 2004
Second printing, July 2004

www.viz.com

store.viz.com

STORY AND ART BY
RUMIKO TAKAH

INUYASHA

VOL. 18   Action Edition

Long ago, in the "Warring States" era of Japan's Muromachi period (*Sengoku-jidai*, approximately 1467-1568 CE), a legendary doglike half-demon called "Inu-Yasha" attempted to steal the Shikon Jewel—or "Jewel of Four Souls"—from a village, but was stopped by the enchanted arrow of the village priestess, Kikyo. Inu-Yasha fell into a deep sleep, pinned to a tree by Kikyo's arrow, while the mortally wounded Kikyo took the Shikon Jewel with her into the fires of her funeral pyre. Years passed.

Fast-forward to the present day. Kagome, a Japanese high-school girl, is pulled into a well one day by a mysterious centipede monster, and finds herself transported into the past, only to come face to face with the trapped Inu-Yasha. She frees him, and Inu-Yasha easily defeats the centipede monster.

The residents of the village, now 50 years older, readily accept Kagome as the reincarnation of their deceased priestess Kikyo, a claim supported by the fact that the Shikon Jewel emerges from a cut on Kagome's body. Unfortunately, the jewel's rediscovery means that the village is soon under attack by a variety of demons in search of this treasure. Then, the jewel is accidentally shattered into many shards, each of which may have the fearsome power of the entire jewel.

Although Inu-Yasha says he hates Kagome because of her resemblance to Kikyo—the woman who "killed" him—he is forced to team up with her when Kaede, the village leader, binds him to Kagome with a powerful spell. Now the two grudging companions must fight to reclaim and reassemble the shattered shards of the Shikon Jewel before they fall into the wrong hands...

THIS VOLUME Inu-Yasha makes a delicate decision to pledge his love and devotion to his special one (at the expense of someone else's feelings for him), while Sango's love for her long-lost little brother jeopardizes the group's safety as the demon Naraku inches closer.

CHARACTERS

KAGOME
Modern-day Japanese schoolgirl who can travel back and forth between the past and present through an enchanted well.

INU-YASHA
Half-demon hybrid, son of a human mother and demon father. His necklace is enchanted, allowing Kagome to control him with a word.

MIROKU
Lecherous Buddhist priest cursed with a mystical "hellhole" in his hand that's slowly killing him.

KOHAKU
Killed by Naraku—but not before first slaying both his own and Sango's father—now he's back again in a newer...if somewhat *slower*...form.

SHIPPO
Orphaned young fox-demon who likes to play shape-changing tricks.

SANGO
"Demon Exterminator" or slayer from the village where the Shikon Jewel was first born.

NARAKU
Enigmatic demon-mastermind behind the miseries of nearly everyone in the story.

KAGURA
Created by Naraku to be his puppet, Kagura can manipulate the dead.

SESSHO-MARU
Inu-Yasha's half-brother, Sessho-Maru is the full-demon son of the same father.

KANNA
Another of Naraku's "offspring," Kanna uses a magic mirror to trap souls.

SCROLL ONE
THE ENEMY
IN THE EARTH

KAGERO-MARU... WHAT WILL YOU DO WITH KAGOME ...!?

I'LL DEVOUR HER... BONES AND ALL.

OH...

I WON'T LET YOU!!

WAH!

HEH HEH HEH... YOU'LL NEVER BE IN TIME.

WH-WHAT...?

PLIP...

MONSTER!!

INU-YASHA...

HOO

INU-YASHA, HE'S...

SWINGING *TETSUSAIGA* ...ONE-HANDED!

HAS HIS BLADE BECOME LIGHTER?

MAYBE THE BLOOD RUSHED TO HIS HEAD AND HE FORGOT HOW HEAVY IT IS...

HE *COULD* BE THAT STUPID, YES.

WHO'S STUPID!?

SIZZLE

HE STILL HAS GOOD HEARING ...

CURSE YOU, KAGERO-MARU...

ESCAPING INTO THE SOIL AGAIN!

KAGOME, ARE YOU ALL RIGHT?

INU-YASHA, YOU'RE BADLY HURT...

SO, THE INSOLENT PUPPY IS STILL ALIVE, EH?

13

KOGA'S LEGS ARE USELESS...

THAT *FOOL* IS *COMPLETELY* USELESS.

INU-YASHA, ARE YOU ALL RIGHT?

BE CAREFUL ...

HMP. YOU KNOW HOW TOUGH I AM!!

DON'T LUMP ME WITH THAT STARVING WOLF!

SOMEDAY THAT ARROGANT PUPPY WILL PAY...

HAH.

KRAK

14

MOVE ASIDE, WOLF!

I'M GONNA SLICE UP JUROMARU!!

TETSUS-AIGA'S HEAVY AGAIN...?

JUST AS I THOUGHT... HE WAS SO INTENT ON PROTECTING LADY KAGOME THAT HE FORGOT...

HA! WHEN YOUR *BRAIN* COMES BACK, YOUR *KNEES* GET WEAK!

WHA...?

SHUT UP!

I'M GONNA SLICE *YOU* UP TOO, WHILE I'M AT IT!

GRIP

I AIN'T GONNA *THANK* YOU!

YOU *OWE* ME NOW!

SHOO---!!

...WHAT IS THIS JUROMARU...?

HE GOT KICKED BY KOGA AND NOT EVEN THE COLOR OF HIS *FACE* CHANGED.

IF THE BATTLE DRAGS ON ANY LONGER, EVEN *INU-YASHA'S* BODY WON'T LAST.

AND KAGEROMARU, WHO'S HIDING WE-DON'T-KNOW-WHERE... IS BOUND TO ATTACK AGAIN.

THAT'S IT!

IF I COULD JUST NULLIFY KAGEROMARU ALONE...

MONK, LEND ME YOUR STAFF!

KWIP

RATTLE

YOU HAVE AN IDEA...?

THIS POISON... IT DOESN'T LAST TOO LONG, BUT...

IT PROBABLY CAN CHASE KAGEROMARU OUT INTO THE OPEN!

HSSSH

TKKK

RATTLE

SHH SIZZLE

SHHH

THE SOIL'S TURNING *RED*...

21

STUPID PUPPY, WHAT DO YOU THINK YOU'RE...!?

TP

KOFF

HNGH...

HUH?

YOU'RE SO *CARELESS*, LITTLE DOGGIE.

HAVE YOU FINALLY BIT THE DUST THIS TIME!?

INU-YASHA-!

DON'T WORRY, KAGOME.

I CAN TAKE CARE OF THE REST ON MY OWN.

EH...?

AS LONG AS KAGEROMARU ISN'T AROUND TO INTERFERE, A DEMON LIKE *THAT* ONE IS NOTHING...

23

! NO SENSE OF KAGEROMARU'S AURA... *AT ALL?!*

IS HE HIDING HIMSELF AMONG THE SHADOWS, OR...?

DON'T TELL ME...

KOGA! *RETREAT,* YOU IDIOT!!

SCROLL TWO
PULVERIZED

26

YOU **DOG.**

MOOSH

YOU WERE PLANNING TO KILL *ME* ALONG *WITH* THEM, WEREN'T YOU !?

.....

TMM

H-HOLD ON...!

...SWINGING YOUR BLADE FULL FORCE LIKE THAT, NOT HOLDING BACK *ONE BIT*!

THAT'S BECAUSE HE KNOWS HOW *FAST* YOU ARE, KOGA! HE *KNEW* YOU'D BE ABLE TO GET OUT OF THE WAY!!

RIGHT, INU-YASHA...??

SNORT YOU'RE ONE TIRESOME WOLF, YOU KNOW THAT?!

IF YOU DON'T SHOW ME SOME RESPECT, I REALLY **WILL** SLICE YOU UP NEXT TIME!

HUH— I'D LIKE TO SEE YOU **TRY**, YOU LUCKY MONGREL!

INU-YASHA, **SIT!**

KOGA, WHY NOT CALL IT QUITS FOR THE DAY?

WHAT ARE YOU TRYING TO PULL, KAGOME?!

YOU HAVE SOME **SERIOUS INJURIES**, YOU KNOW.

IF YOU FIGHT ANY MORE RIGHT **NOW**...

KOGA, THANK YOU FOR TODAY, REALLY.

THANKS TO YOU, WE WON. WE'RE GRATEFUL.

BLAH YADA BLAH

NOT TERRIBLY **CONVINCING**, IS SHE?

SOMEHOW I DON'T THINK THIS WILL GET KOGA TO LEAVE...

KAGO-ME...

STARE

MM...?

YOU ARE MY MATE.

I CAN'T LEAVE YOU IN THAT USELESS PUPPY'S CARE **ALL** THE TIME, YOU KNOW.

UH...

SKWEEZ

DON'T YOU GET *TIRED* OF THIS—!?

WHENEVER YOU'RE IN DANGER, I WILL *ALWAYS* COME TO RESCUE YOU.

WELL, THEN.

POP POP POP POP

TILL NEXT TIME.

OH.

HE LEFT...?

WAIT, YOU FLEA-BITTEN—!

KROUCH

SIT!

UGH.

...YOU—YOU LET *KOGA* GET AWAY AGAIN, YOU...!

INU-YASHA... IN YOUR CURRENT STATE...

DO YOU REALLY THINK THAT CUR COULD EVER **BEAT** ME!?

.....

LOOK... LET'S JUST GET THOSE WOUNDS TREATED.

I TOLD YOU, I DON'T NEED IT!

SO, WHAT **WAS** THAT JUST NOW, HUH? THIS ATTITUDE OF YOURS!

FLATTERING AND PRANCING AROUND THAT FLEABAG.

IT WAS SO DISGUSTING, I COULDN'T WATCH.

I MEAN, TO BEGIN WITH, YOU'RE SO...

.....

RRRRMMBLE FLINCH!

WH-WHY ARE YOU *LOOKING* AT ME LIKE THAT....?

B-BMP B-BMP B-BMP

I'M GOING HOME.

HUH...?

I'M GOING BACK TO THE ERA I BELONG IN!

FINE— GO HOME!

I'M NOT GONNA STOP YOU!

NOW THAT YOU TWO HAVE SETTLED THINGS, SHALL WE GET GOING?

I'D LIKE TO GET OUR LORD MONK'S WOUNDS PROPERLY TREATED, TOO...

FLUTTER
FLUTTER

HSSH...

NARAKU,
EH...?

NOW
WHAT.

...HO.

HSSH...

YOUR
INSTINCTS
ARE RAZOR-
SHARP AS
USUAL,
KIKYO.

DID YOU THINK I WOULDN'T NOTICE?

AND NOT JUST TODAY...

YOU'VE BEEN COMING BY COUNTLESS TIMES TO CHECK ON ME.

HMMM...

IT SEEMS I CAN'T LET MY GUARD DOWN AROUND YOU.

KIKYO **DESPISES** THE DEMON NARAKU.

SHE IS A DANGEROUS WOMAN TO KEEP ALIVE.

AND YET...

NAR-AKU... I DON'T THINK I REALIZED...

...HOW STRONGLY, INSIDE YOU...

...ONIGUMO'S HEART STILL BEATS.

"ONIGUMO'S HEART," YOU SAY?!

THIS−?!

SCROLL THREE
KIKYO'S CRISIS

RRRG! INU-YASHA, YOU JERK!

I ONLY STOPPED YOU FROM FIGHTING BECAUSE I WAS **WORRIED** ABOUT YOUR INJURIES!

WAIT, KAGOME.

THIS IS JUST INU-YASHA'S USUAL JEALOUSY, RIGHT?

SHIPPO...

KAGOME, YOU ARE MY MATE.

HE'S INSECURE, IS ALL, SO HE CAN'T HELP TAKING KOGA'S SILLINESS SERIOUSLY.

IT'S KIND OF PATHETIC HOW HE CAN'T **BELIEVE** IN HIMSELF.

AND ON TOP OF THAT, HE **DOES** LOVE YOU...

...I KNOW.

DON'T WORRY, I'LL BE RIGHT BACK.

I'M JUST GOING TO PICK UP SOME MODERN MEDICINE AND BRING IT HERE.

EH...? THAT *BLACK CLOUD*...

HSSH...

IT'S BEEN HOVERING O'ER THE TEMPLE FOR A TIME NOW...

.....

IT'S AN *OMEN*, IT IS...

FLICKER

FLICKER

THOSE LIGHTS... THE **SOULS** OF THE **DEAD**.

IS THAT "THING"...

...*DEVOURING* THOSE SOULS?!

HAH ...!?

WHAT *IS* THAT THING!?

NARAKU...
...IS DECLARING *WAR* ON ME.

HOW STRONGLY, INSIDE YOU...

...ONIGUMO'S HEART STILL BEATS.

ONIGUMO'S HEART...

THAT FILTHY *BANDIT*...

THOUGH COMPLETELY PARALYZED, HE LET HIS *BASE THOUGHTS* RUN WILD TOWARD KIKYO...

TO TAKE HER, HE OFFERED HIS BODY UP TO A HORDE OF DEMONS...

...AND GAVE *BIRTH* TO *NARAKU.*

THAT STUPID MORTAL HEART...

THAT *HEART* THAT *LUSTS* AFTER KIKYO...

...STILL *REMAINS* WITHIN THIS BODY—!?

HUH. ABSURD.

KIKYO, YOU'VE MOCKED ME LONG ENOUGH.

NOW THAT I HAVE MOST OF THE SHIKON JEWEL IN MY POSSESSION...

...I HAVE NO MORE USE FOR YOU.

YOUR TIME HAS COME, KIKYO.

NOW, NARAKU RETURNS YOU TO THE UNDERWORLD FOREVERMORE.

UHHH...

THAT DEMON...

PLANNING TO *DEVOUR* ALL THE SOULS IN THIS LAND.

AND IF ALL THE DEAD SOULS ARE GONE... MY BODY WILL MOVE NO LONGER.

I MUST *DESTROY* HIM WHILE I STILL HAVE THE STRENGTH TO DRAW MY BOW...

KREE'''

N...NO...

WOBBLE

SOULS... BEING SUCKED *OUT* OF ME...

FLUTTER FLUTTER

INU-YASHA... DON'T YOU HAVE ANY INTENTION OF GOING AND PICKING UP LADY KAGOME?

SHUT IT. I'M *HAPPIER* WITH HER GONE.

WELL THEN, CAN YOU START *ACTING* HAPPY?

I'M TIRED OF YOUR SULK.

LADY KAGOME'S PATIENCE BECOMES MORE ADMIRABLE ALL THE TIME, DOES IT NOT...?

I WAS *JUST* THINKING THAT.

55

HSSH...

THAT SCENT... A DEMON?!

SNIFF

FLAP FLAP FLAP

!

56

SCROLL FOUR
ONIGUMO'S HEART

NO ONE IS GOING TO KILL KIKYO!!

KIKYO, HOLD ONTO ME TIGHT!

WHOA!

THAT DEMON... HE'LL STEAL ALL THE *DEAD SOULS* THAT ANIMATE KIKYO'S BODY...

HOO—!

HSSH

YOU MONSTER *BUG.*

IT'S GOOD I HAPPENED TO BE HERE...

HSSH

PAP

PAP

JUST YOU WAIT, KIKYO...

YOUR CREATURES WILL GO AND GATHER SOULS FOR YOU...

INU... YASHA...?

KIKYO!

YOU CAN SPEAK?!

WHY...

...ARE YOU HERE?

THAT'S *MY* LINE.

WHAT ARE *YOU* DOING HERE?

WHAT!?

HWIP

NIGHT **ALREADY!?**

AARGH! WHY DIDN'T YOU WAKE ME!?

'CAUSE YOU WERE STILL **ASLEEP.**

50 YEARS AGO... IN THIS PLACE...

I SHOT YOU IN THE CHEST WITH AN ARROW...

AND THEN *MY* LIFE ENDED, TOO.

YEAH...

KIKYO...WHY ARE YOU BRINGING THIS UP NOW...?

INU-YASHA...

WHY DO YOU THINK NARAKU ENSNARED BOTH OF US IN HIS TRAPS... AND MADE US *HATE* EACH OTHER...?

IT WAS...

...TO CORRUPT THE *SHIKON JEWEL*.

TO STAIN YOUR *"HEART"*– WHICH COULD *"CLEANSE"* THE JEWEL, WITH *"HATRED"*...

HMPH...

BUT... HE DIDN'T HAVE TO.

EVEN *WITHOUT* CORRUPTING MY HEART...

JUST THE **TOUCH** OF NARAKU'S EVIL AURA...

...SHOULD HAVE BEEN SUFFICIENT TO **CORRUPT** THE JEWEL.

KIKYO... WHAT ARE YOU TRYING TO SAY?!

IT WAS ONIGUMO'S **HEART**, STILL BURNING INSIDE NARAKU...

...THAT TORE US **APART**.

ONIGUMO'S HEART...?!

THAT BANDIT... WANTED TO MAKE ME HIS WOMAN.

72

IT WAS THE BANDIT'S DEVOURING JEALOUSY...

...THAT PLOTTED TO MAKE ME *KILL* YOU BY MY OWN HAND...

JEALOUSY...?

BUT THAT'S ABSURD...

YES, IT *IS* ABSURD.

AND IT... IS ALSO *HUMAN*.

.....

INSIDE NARAKU... IS ONIGUMO'S HEART...!?

HE DOESN'T WANT TO SEE IT...

...BUT I BELIEVE THOSE FEELINGS FOR ME STILL REMAIN.

WAIT, KIKYO.

THAT MEANS *NARAKU*...!

AND SO, IN AN ATTEMPT TO *DESTROY* THOSE FEELINGS...

...HE TRIED TO *KILL* ME.

NGH...

GRRR

I'M **NOT** GOING TO HAND YOU OVER TO THE LIKES OF **HIM!**

INU-YASHA...

YIKES.

I AM SOOO **LATE...!**

...WELL, AT LEAST...

...BY NOW HE'S HAD TIME TO GET THINGS STRAIGHT.

POP

FUMP

HUH...?

GLEAM

SCROLL FIVE
JEALOUSY

NARAKU'S LAIR.

YOU KNOW WHERE IT IS, DON'T YOU?

AND IF I DO...?

IT'S OBVIOUS.

I'D RIDE IN THERE, AND...

I'D SLAUGHTER THE DEMON!

THEN, KIKYO...

YOU WOULDN'T NEED TO FIGHT ANY MORE.

.....

I TOLD YOU, INU-YASHA.

I AM THE ONLY ONE WHO CAN EXORCISE NARAKU FROM THE REALM OF THE LIVING FOREVER.

BUT...

IF HE **ATTACKS** YOU LIKE HE JUST DID...

WHO WILL PROTECT YOU?!

I'M THE ONLY ONE YOU HAVE!!

INU-YASHA...

I WON'T LET YOU HAND YOUR LIFE OVER TO HIM AGAIN!

INU-YASHA, PLEASE...

I WON'T LEAVE MYSELF VULNERABLE LIKE THIS EVER AGAIN.

BESIDES, NARAKU CAN'T KILL ME.

NOT SO LONG AS *ONIGUMO'S HEART* IS STILL IN HIM... AND STILL YEARNS FOR ME.

WHAT?

ONIGUMO'S HEART... IN NARAKU...?

THAT MEANS...

NARAKU LOVES *KIKYO*?!

SO *THAT'S* WHAT INU-YASHA IS SO WORKED UP ABOUT...

B-BMP B-BMP B-BMP

I'M GOING TO GO NOW...

KIKYO!

GO, INU-YASHA...

RETURN TO YOUR COMPANIONS.

.....

SHK...

INU-YASHA...

THAT TIME, WHEN THE SOULS WERE PULLED FROM ME AND I BECAME WEAK...

I THOUGHT I WAS GOING TO MEET MY END ALONE.

BUT YOU...

YOU WERE THERE FOR ME, INU-YASHA.

I WAS SO HAPPY...

KIKYO...

ZSH

GRIP

IF ANYTHING HAPPENS, CALL FOR ME!

INU-YASHA...

SHK...

JEALOUSY ...?

IS THIS, TOO, PART OF ONIGUMO'S...

...GRUBBY LITTLE HUMAN HEART...?

BAH.

GNG

LORD... ?

RIP RIP RIP

EH?!

HSSH...

DANGLE

TH-
THE **SKIN**
OFF HIS
BACK...?!

YEEE!

ARE YOU GOING MAD?

.....

SHP

OOOSH

WHAT IS THE MATTER, NARAKU?

SILENCE.

JUST CLEAN IT UP.

HSSH...

LADY KAEDE, WHAT ARE...?

.....

SOULS OF THE DEAD.

GLEEN!

KIKYO... ELDER SISTER...

ARE YOU NEAR?

90

KIKYO...

!

KAGOME...!

SO SHE
SAW IT
ALL...?

HOW CAN HE JUST STAND THERE WITHOUT LOOKING AWAY?!

HSSH...

SHHk...

THIS IS THE CAVE WHERE I GAVE SHELTER TO THE WOUNDED BANDIT ONIGUMO...

THAT'S RIGHT, ONIGUMO.

THIS IS WHERE YOU LAY...

HSS...

EVEN IF I TEAR OFF THE SKIN... OR BURN IT WITH FIRE...

THE *SPIDER* ON MY BACK ALWAYS RETURNS.

IT NEVER DISAPPEARS...

...JUST LIKE ONIGUMO'S HEART.

SCROLL SIX

THE SOIL SHIELD

NARAKU...

DID YOU THINK THAT IF YOU JUST KILLED ME...

...YOU COULD BE FREED FROM THE MORTAL HEART THAT *YEARNS* FOR ME?.

...AND WHAT IF I DID?

HA. YOU WON'T BE ABLE TO TAKE MY LIFE...

KREEE

...NOT NOW, NOT EVER!

YOU'RE QUITE THE PRETENDER YOURSELF, KIKYO.

HERE I WAS THINKING YOU WERE MEEKLY CLINGING TO INU-YASHA'S ARM...

...AND SUDDENLY YOU RIDE INTO THIS CASTLE.

YOU WERE SPYING ON US WHEN INU-YASHA RESCUED ME, WEREN'T YOU?

YOU SCUM...

HMPH. I WAS ONLY HOPING TO WATCH YOU DIE.

KIKYO...

DO YOU THINK YOU CAN JUST RIDE IN AND OUT OF HERE?

BURBLE

UUP

!

THIS DEMON IS YOUR REVENANT...

UNDERSTAND, NARAKU?

IF EVEN A SINGLE FINGER TOUCHES ME, *THIS* IS WHAT WILL HAPPEN TO YOU, TOO!

THE DEMONIC POWER WAS DISSOLVED...

A SHIELD...!?

THE SOIL FROM THE CAVE WHERE YOU LAY, WHEN YOU WERE THE BANDIT **ONIGUMO**...

NARAKU...

IT IS STEEPED IN YOUR FOUL DESIRES.

SO YOU'VE ARMED YOURSELF WITH THE CAVE DIRT?

YES.

ONIGUMO DIDN'T WANT MY DEATH.

HIS DESIRE WILL PROTECT ME.

IF YOU TOUCH THE SOIL-SHIELD, ONIGUMO'S HEART WILL FLOW INTO YOU...

...AND IT WILL **STEAL AWAY** YOUR DEMONIC POWER.

REMEMBER THIS, NARAKU: *YOU CAN- NOT KILL ME.*

YOU REMAIN A MERE *HALF- DEMON.*

SHF

AS LONG AS YOU CONTAIN A *HUMAN HEART...*

YOU REMAIN A MERE *HALF- DEMON.*

YES... AND *THAT* IS WHY...

I SEEK TO BECOME A *FULL* DEMON.

AND THIS... UM... FIGHTS INFECTION.

I BROUGHT PLENTY OF GAUZE AND ROLLS OF BANDAGES, TOO.

WELL, THEN... I'M GONNA GET GOING, OK?

EH...? KAGOME...?

YOU'RE GOING BACK TO YOUR WORLD AGAIN?

OH. YEAH.

I JUST CAME TO DELIVER THE MEDICINES, SO...

BUT- AREN'T YOU GOING TO MAKE UP WITH INU-YASHA?

IT WAS SUCH A PETTY QUARREL...

OH... THAT'S RIGHT.

I WAS FIGHTING WITH INU-YASHA, WASN'T I...?

I'D COMPLETELY FORGOTTEN...

I'M THE ONLY ONE YOU HAVE!!

WHO WILL PROTECT YOU!?

HEY, MONK.

KAGOME DIDN'T SEEM VERY CHEERFUL, DID SHE?

NO...

WELL...

IT'S NOT AS IF WE CAN'T GUESS WHAT IT'S ABOUT.

SHK...

INU-YASHA...

ZIPP

OH...

INU-YASHA, LADY KAGOME HAS RETURNED AGAIN TO HER OWN LAND.

.....

I SEE...

INU-YASHA, YOU...

YOU MET UP WITH THE LADY KIKYO AGAIN, RIGHT?

109

BACK
THERE...

INU-YASHA
NEVER
TOOK
HIS EYES
OFF MINE.

HE WAS TRYING TO SAY SOMETHING, BUT...

...I WAS TOO SCARED TO HEAR IT, AND RAN AWAY.

INU-YASHA'S ALREADY...

HE'S MADE HIS DECISION.

INU-YASHA AND KIKYO STARTED HATING EACH OTHER BECAUSE OF NARAKU'S TRAP.

AND THEN KIKYO...

...DIED IN ORDER TO FOLLOW HIM.

111

NOW NARAKU, WHO TORE THE TWO OF THEM APART...

...HAS COME AFTER KIKYO AGAIN.

I'M THE ONLY ONE YOU HAVE!!

WHO WILL PROTECT YOU!?

FOR ME TO SQUEEZE IN BETWEEN THEM...

THERE'S NO ROOM.

KAGOME,
I'M SORRY..

FLAP

I CAN'T
LEAVE
KIKYO
ALONE,
AFTER
ALL...

I
CAN'T...

AND
SO...

KAGOME
I CAN'T
SEE YOU
ANYMORE.

I
MUSTN'T
SEE YOU
ANYMORE.

KIKYO
SACRIFICED
HER LIFE FOR
INU-YASHA'S
SAKE.

I CAN'T
COMPETE
AGAINST
THAT.

I CAN'T
GO BACK TO
INU-YASHA'S
SIDE EVER
AGAIN.

SCROLL SEVEN
WHERE THEY FIRST MET

INU-YASHA WON'T BE COMING TO GET ME ANYMORE.

BUT...

THE SHIKON SHARDS... I'VE BROUGHT THEM BACK TO THE PRESENT...

WHAT SHOULD I DO...?

I SHOULD RETURN THEM.

YEAH. ONCE I DO THAT...

YOU KNOW! THE RELATIONSHIP BETWEEN YOU AND THAT GUY WHO GETS VIOLENTLY JEALOUS EVEN WHILE HE'S DOUBLE-DIPPING ON YOU!

SO'D YOU *DUMP* HIM, OR...?

FLINCH!

...HUH?

SH-HH

KAGO-ME?

DID I... SAY SOMETHING I SHOULDN'T HAVE?

ZZZZZIP

B-BMP B-BMP B-BMP

SIGH

I THINK *I* GOT DUMPED.

WHIRL

WHAT...?

...THAT MEANS...

SHE GOT DUMPED?!

SHE STILL *LIKES* THAT CREEP...?

B-BAMP B-BAMP B-BAMP

BUT IT'S OKAY...

I'M ALL RIGHT NOW, REALLY.

...*HE* DUMPED *YOU?*

YEAH... BUT...

UM... UM...

DON'T ASK ME ANYTHING MORE, OKAY?

I'M FINE. I AM.

...MEANING, DON'T RUB ANY MORE *SALT* INTO THE *WOUND*, HUH?

SCARY...

THAT *FAKE SMILE* OF HERS IS *SCARY!*

I CAN'T BELIEVE YOU, INU-YASHA!

FLAP...

YOU GET FURIOUS AT KAGOME FOR JUST ACTING *FRIENDLY* WITH KIGA...

...THEN *YOU* GET BACK TOGETHER WITH *KIKYO*?!

...AMAZING, ISN'T HE?

.....

INU-YASHA, GO SEE LADY KAGOME.

SHUT UP.

I SWORE TO MYSELF I'D NEVER CHASE KAGOME AGAIN.

DON'T MISUNDERSTAND ME.

WROOO

I'M TELLING YOU TO GO RETRIEVE THE *SHIKON SHARDS* THAT LADY KAGOME'S TAKEN BACK TO HER LAND.

YOU'RE THE ONLY ONE OF US WHO CAN PASS THROUGH THAT MAGIC WELL.

WHA...

JUST THE SHIKON SHARDS...?

YOU DON'T CARE ABOUT KAGOME AT ALL?!

IT CAN'T BE HELPED, CAN IT?

INU-YASHA HAS CHOSEN LADY KIKYO.

IT WOULD BE CRUEL FOR HIM TO ASK LADY KAGOME TO RETURN.

INU-YASHA... ARE YOU CERTAIN THAT'S WHAT YOU WANT?

AGH! YOU *TOO*, OLD LADY?!

THE KIKYO YOU NOW KNOW IS BUT A CONSTRUCT OF BONE AND SOIL.

MY SISTER HAS NO BUSINESS BEING ALIVE.

BUT... IT'S STILL KIKYO'S *SOUL*...

SHFF...

THE SHIKON SHARDS...

I'VE GOT TO TAKE THEM BACK.

BUT...

I DON'T WANT TO.

I'M AFRAID.

AFRAID IF I GIVE THEM BACK...

...I WON'T BE ABLE TO SEE INU-YASHA ANYMORE.

KAGOME, I'M SORRY...

I CAN'T LEAVE KIKYO ALONE—

I DON'T WANT TO HEAR IT!

I DON'T...

KIKYO...

125

I MUST LOOK HATEFUL RIGHT NOW.

I CAN'T SEE INU-YASHA LOOKING LIKE THIS...

GLINT...

THE SHARDS...

HSSH...

THE SACRED TREE.

THAT'S RIGHT... THIS SAME TREE...

THIS IS WHERE INU-YASHA WAS SEALED...

...OVER 500 YEARS AGO.

THIS IS WHERE I FIRST MET HIM.

BUT WHY DID WE HAVE TO MEET?

SCROLL EIGHT
KAGOME'S HEART

SCROLL EIGHT
KAGOME'S HEART

...WOULD MEAN SAYING *GOODBYE* TO HER.

I'VE GOT TO TELL HER...

...WHAT I COULDN'T SAY BACK THEN.

INU-YASHA. YOU'RE HERE, AFTER ALL.

LONG TIME NO SEE, LORD INU-YASHA

...THE CASTLE DISAPPEARED? WHAT DO YOU MEAN?

JUST AS IT SOUNDS.

GONE WITHOUT A TRACE, AS IF IT HAD BEEN GOUGED OUT BY A DEMON'S TALONS...

...AND FROM THAT SITE FLEW A COUNTLESS HORDE OF *WINGED CREATURES,* LIKE INSECTS.

INSECTS ?!

WERE THEY NARAKU'S UNHOLY WASPS...

...THE SAIMYŌSHŌ?!

MOST LIKELY.

SANGO AND I WILL LEAVE FIRST THING IN THE MORNING TO INVESTIGATE THE REMAINS OF THE CASTLE.

INU-YASHA, WHAT ABOUT YOU?

WHAT ABOUT—!? I'M GOING, OF COURSE!

ALL RIGHT, BUT WHAT OF KAGOME?

HUH? WHAT...?

NEVER *MIND* KAGOME!

WHAT WILL YOU GAIN BY PUTTING IT OFF?

IF YOUR HEART IS DECIDED, YOU SHOULD GO AND SEE HER.

HE'S *ALWAYS* EAGER TO PUT IT OFF...

WHY, YOU—

WHY ARE YOU TWO SO DESPERATE TO COME BETWEEN ME AND KAGOME?!

YOU DON'T **WANT** US TO...?

UH

IT'S...

IT'S NOT **ABOUT** WHAT I WANT.

I HAVE TO PROTECT KIKYO.

AND THAT MEANS...

I CAN NEVER ASK KAGOME TO COME BACK!

HEY, WHERE'D THEY GO?

THAT'S HOW IT IS...

I CAN NEVER ASK HER.

BUT KAGOME SHOULD HEAR THAT FROM ME.

I'LL GO.

I'VE GOT TO SEE HER AND BID HER FAREWELL... OR ELSE...

I'LL NEVER BE ABLE TO MOVE ON.

...KAGOME...

BACK IN MY OWN TIME...

I THOUGHT ABOUT THINGS.

ABOUT YOU AND KIKYO AND...

...ABOUT ME.

KAGO-ME...

I...

I KNOW.

I FINALLY UNDERSTAND YOUR FEELINGS, AND...

AND I DIDN'T THINK I COULD STAY IN THIS TIME ANY LONGER.

KAGOME...

UNTIL I MET YOU,

BUT YOU CRIED, FOR MY SAKE...

YOU STAYED BY MY SIDE.

I COULDN'T TRUST ANYONE.

I FEEL LIGHTER WITH YOU.

MY HEART IS CALM.

BUT...

I CAN'T *AFFORD* LIGHTNESS OR PEACE.

NOT WHEN...

NOT WHEN KIKYO *DIED* CHASING AFTER ME.

145

I'M STILL ALIVE.

I THOUGHT A LOT ABOUT KIKYO.

SHE AND I ARE NOT AT ALL ALIKE.

EVEN IF I *AM* SOME REINCARNATION OF HER...

I'M STILL NOT REALLY KIKYO.

MY HEART IS MINE.

BUT, YOU KNOW, THERE *IS* ONE THING...

...SHE AND I HAVE IN COMMON.

JUST LIKE ME...

SHE
COULDN'T
BEAR NOT
TO SEE
YOU
AGAIN.

SOMEHOW, IF I THINK OF IT THAT WAY... THAT KIKYO FELT THE SAME WAY *I* DO...

IT'S EASIER.

I DON'T HAVE TO HATE HER SO MUCH.

SO I DUG UP THE COURAGE...

...TO COME AND SEE YOU.

KAGOME...

I WANTED TO SEE YOU, TOO.

BUT...

I... I WANT TO STAY WITH YOU.

I WON'T BE ABLE TO FORGET YOU.

KAGOME...

I...

I DON'T KNOW HOW TO ANSWER.

INU-YASHA...

JUST TELL ME ONE THING.

YEAH...?

SHK...

YOU... WANT TO STAY...?

.....

YES.

I CAN'T EVER BREAK THE BOND BETWEEN INU-YASHA AND KIKYO.

I KNOW THAT.

BUT, INU-YASHA...

I ALSO KNOW...

...THAT IT WAS NO ACCIDENT YOU AND I MET.

I CAN'T LEAVE YOU NOW.

LET'S GO, INU-YASHA.

...YEAH...

IT'S ALL RIGHT TO BE LIGHT, SOMETIMES.

I WANT YOU TO LAUGH.

I DON'T KNOW WHAT I MIGHT BE ABLE TO DO, BUT...

I'LL ALWAYS BE NEAR YOU.

SCROLL NINE
THE CASTLE'S GHOST

I WAS WORRIED...

I THOUGHT YOU WERE NEVER COMING BACK, KAGOME!

I'M SORRY, SHIPPO.

HEY, INU-YASHA.

YOU BETTER HAVE APOLOGIZED TO HER *GOOD*.

OH, SHUT UP.

I WONDER HOW THOSE TWO SETTLED THINGS.

WELL, I WOULD IMAGINE...

...THAT LADY KAGOME MUST HAVE MET HIM HALFWAY.

YOU MEAN, SHE *FORGAVE* HIM FOR GOING WITH KIKYO?!

156

...I DON'T BUY IT.

I THOUGHT KAGOME WAS MADE OF STRONGER STUFF.

YOU *SAW* HOW LONG AND HARD INU-YASHA BROODED ON IT.

SHE MAY HAVE UNDERSTOOD THAT PRESSURING HIM WOULDN'T GAIN MUCH.

NOT THAT THERE WAS MUCH TO *GAIN* IN THE *FIRST* PLACE.

STARE—

AN' WHAT'RE *YOU* LOOKIN' AT?!

AT LEAST HE SHOWS *SOME* GUILT OVER IT...

EVEN SO...

THERE'S NOTHING LEFT OF THE CASTLE.

ARE WE *SURE* THERE EVEN *WAS* A CASTLE HERE...?

IT'S TRUE, NOW THAT YOU'VE SAID IT...

WE *HAVE* BEEN LURED TO FALSE CASTLES OFTEN ENOUGH.

...SANGO?

.....

159

IT'S NO TRICK.

NARAKU'S CASTLE **WAS** HERE.

EH...?

SANGO... THAT'S...

...MY FATHER'S ARMOUR, YES.

HH...

THAT DAY... WE DEMON-SLAYERS WERE LURED TO NARAKU'S CASTLE...

FATHER AND ALL HIS COMPANIONS HAD BEEN SLAUGHTERED...

...AND THE TRICK HAD BEEN PLAYED ON MY YOUNGER BROTHER, KOHAKU.

HIS SOUL HAD BEEN *SEIZED* BY NARAKU.

...THE BODIES WERE BURIED IN THE CORNER OF THE CASTLE GARDEN.

IT WAS HERE.

OH, SANGO...

161

LORD MIROKU...?

WSSH

WE MUST NOT LEAVE THE REMAINS IN SUCH AN ABOMINABLE PLACE.

HWAH

LORD MONK.

I SHALL TAKE THEM TO HOLY GROUND AND HOLD SERVICE.

SHH

WILL THAT BE SATISFACTORY TO YOU, SANGO?

DIG

YES...

THANK YOU, LORD MONK.

IF THIS **WAS** NARAKU'S CASTLE...

...WHERE ARE THE PEOPLE WHO **LIVED** HERE?

WHERE'S SANGO'S LITTLE BROTHER? WAS HE...

...DESTROYED, ALONG WITH THE BUILDING?

WSSH

HYOON

NOT WHERE YE'VE COME FROM?

NOT YOUR PEOPLE, OR EVEN YER OWN *NAME?*

M.... MAYBE...

MAYBE YE LIVED AT THE *CASTLE...?*

CASTLE?

10 DAYS GONE, LORD HITOMI'S CASTLE *VANISHED,* AS IF THE SPIRITS THEMSELVES TOOK IT.

AND IT WAS THE VERY NEXT DAY THAT WE FOUND YE LYIN' IN THE ROAD.

COULD BE SOMETHING SO BAD HAPPENED...

...THAT YE, BLESS YER HEART, CAN'T REMEMBER A THING.

CASTLE
...

THAT'S
RIGHT,
I...

...I
WAS
IN A
CASTLE...

OLD WOMAN...
OLD MAN!

...EH?

I'VE GOTTA GO.

GO— GO— GO WHERE...?!

I CAN'T *STAY* HERE!

IT'S DANGEROUS! DON'T GO OUTSIDE, NO MATTER WHAT!

THANKS FOR EVERYTHING!

OH...

I *ESCAPED* FROM THE CASTLE.

THAT NIGHT...

THE CASTLE DISAPPEARED.

YES— I REMEMBER NOW!

KOHAKU...
I HAVE
NO MORE
NEED TO
KEEP YOU
ALIVE.

GO JOIN
YOUR FATHER
AND HIS
COMPANIONS.

"KOHAKU"...?

MY
NAME...
IS KOHAKU?

SHK

THIS
WAY?!

I CAN FEEL THE SHIKON SHARD... IT'S CLOSE... AND IT'S *MOVING!*

! BZZ!

SAIMYŌ-SHŌ?!

KGH!

THEY'RE AFTER THE SHARD, TOO?!

!

SHH!

RRR!

SPLIT

WAAH!

B-BOOM

HEH HEH HEH... KOHAKU...

DON'T YOU **KNOW** YOU MUST DIE?

NOW... COME **BACK** TO ME. BRING THE SHARD...

...OF THE **SHIKON**, IMPLANTED IN YOUR BODY.

THE... SHIKON SHARD?!

171

SCROLL TEN
KOHAKU'S MEMORY

HEH HEH HEH...

BYOOO

DIE, KOHAKU!

NGH!

THD

!

SHK

GLEEM

THAT DEMON...

IT'S TRYING TO TAKE KOHAKU'S *SHIKON SHARD!*

WHAT?!

KOHAKU IS *ALIVE* BECAUSE OF THE *SHARD* IMPLANTED IN HIS *BODY!*

IF THE
SHARD IS
REMOVED...

KOHAKU
WILL
DIE!

BOOMERANG
BONE!

.....

KOHAKU
...

YOUR SOUL WAS *STOLEN* BY NARAKU...

YOU WERE SUPPOSED TO HAVE BEEN IN NARAKU'S CASTLE.

THEN WHY...?

YOU...

YOU **KNOW** ME?

WHAT...?

YOU HAVE A WOUND ON YOUR ARM...?

LET ME SEE IT.

.....

UH...

HM...?

HAVE WE MET BEFORE?

SO... KOHAKU?

YOU REALLY DON'T RECALL ANYTHING...

...FROM BEFORE YOU ESCAPED THE CASTLE?

I'M SORRY...

...NO.

SURELY YOU REMEMBER NARAKU!

NARAKU...?

KOHAKU... I HAVE NO MORE NEED TO KEEP YOU ALIVE.

GO JOIN YOUR FATHER AND HIS COMPANIONS.

WAS THAT...

...NARAKU...?

...I DON'T LIKE IT.

HE'S PLAY-ACTING. NARAKU'S STILL GOT HIM.

...AND YET IT DOESN'T SEEM SO.

YOU TRUST HIM?

IT'S NOT SO SIMPLE.

IT'S JUST... WHEN KOHAKU APPEARED TO US BEFORE, HE SEEMED...

...LIKE A MARIONETTE. AS IF HE'D HAD HIS *SOUL* EXCISED.

BUT NOW...

I WONDER IF IT'S ALL RIGHT TO LEAVE THE TWO OF THEM ALONE.

SANGO SAID THAT'S THE WAY SHE WANTED IT...

.....

...THE SLAYER'S VILLAGE?

YES. WHERE WE ALL ONCE LIVED.

THEN *I* WAS SLAYING DEMONS, TOO...?

YOU HAD JUST BEGUN.

JUST BEGUN— BECAUSE THE DAY WE WERE SUMMONED TO NARAKU'S CASTLE...

...IT WAS YOUR FIRST MISSION.

IMMEDIATELY YOUR SOUL WAS STOLEN BY NARAKU...

...AND YOU, KOHAKU...

...KILLED OUR FATHER.

PLEASE.

TELL ME EVERYTHING YOU KNOW.

IT'S LONELY LIKE THIS...

NOT KNOWING *WHY* I AM *WHO* I AM.

SIGH...

HE'S... MY BROTHER AGAIN.

GENTLE... A LITTLE TIMID...

YOU'LL NEED TO REMEMBER THINGS BIT BY BIT.

WE'LL BE TOGETHER FROM NOW ON. I'LL HELP YOU.

KOHAKU IS BACK.

HE'S FREE OF NARAKU'S GRASP...

THANK YOU...

...OR SO I'M CHOOSING TO BELIEVE.

BUT... IT'S EMBARRAS-SING...

WHY ARE YOU BLUSHING? I'M YOUR SISTER.

...PEH. IF WE SMACK HIM A FEW TIMES, I BET HE'LL SHOW HIS TRUE CHARACTER.

INU-YASHA, SHAME ON YOU!!

IF ONLY IT WERE THAT SIMPLE.

HER LITTLE BROTHER HAS RETURNED...

...JUST AS HE WAS. BUT COULD *THAT* BE THE TRAP?

YEAH...

BUT IF IT IS, THEN SANGO'S IN DANGER.

NARAKU *DOES* LOVE PLAYING WITH PEOPLE'S EMOTIONS...

EH ?!

PWIK

...A
SWARM...

IT'S
COMING...
...AND
IT'S...

WSH

WSH

BUZZ

THE SAIMYŌ-SHŌ...

NARAKU'S "WASP" AGENTS.

WHOA!

KAGURA!

YOU'RE SHELTERING KOHAKU, AREN'T YOU?

BRING HIM OUT.

WHAT—?!

DON'T PLAY IGNORANT WITH ME.

KOHAKU. THE LITTLE MONSTER *NARAKU* WAS KEEPING AROUND.

HE RAN OFF DURING THE MAYHEM...

...WITH THE *SHIKON SHARD* STILL EMBEDDED IN HIS BODY!

.....

AND *YOU'VE* COME TO TAKE HIM *BACK*..?

FEH.

ALL NARAKU WANTS IS THE *SHARD.*

THE *CORPSE,* HIS BELOVED SISTER IS WELCOME TO.

YOU...!

HAH!

KOHA-KU?

I'M THE ONE THEY WANT.

IF I GO OUT ALONE...

HSH

GNG

KOHAKU!

NO WAY. YOU'RE *NOT* LEAVING ME AGAIN.

YOU'RE MY ONLY LITTLE BROTHER.

.....

HEH.

AND SO THEY BEGIN TO ACT OUT THE PLAY THAT NARAKU HAS WRITTEN.

PLAY IT WELL, KOHAKU!

TO BE CONTINUED▷